Energy Mandalas
of Crystals and Stones

Gail Alexander

IbbiLane Press
Copyright © 2016
All rights reserved. No part of this book may be reproduced or utilized in any form or by any means, electronic or mechanical, including photocopying, recording, or by any information storage and retrieval systems without the permission in writing from the publisher.

Cover design by the author.

ISBN-13: 978-0692781456 (IbbiLane Press)

ISBN-10: 0692781455

Dedication

To my mother: Thank you for teaching me to love gemstones and crystals at an early age. You will always be with me. I love you!

Acknowledgements

To all my friends: Thank you for helping me through a difficult time of my life. Thank you for all your support, caring and presence in my life.

To my family and extended family: Thank you for your support over the last couple of months.

To my friend Vicki: Who shared a love of collecting or hoarding crystals as much as I do. I miss our conversations and I miss you.

To my friend Bill: Thank you for all the gifts you shared with me. I miss you.

To Kellie: Thank you for your constant belief in me and for my vision with this book. I am grateful and appreciative.

To all the crystals and gemstones: Thank you for the gift you bring into my life on a daily bases.

Table of Contents

Introduction	9
Black and Red Energy Mandalas of Crystals and Stones	11
Hematite	12
Shungite	14
Black Tourmaline	16
Garnet	18
Orange Energy Mandalas of Crystals and Stones	21
Tangerine Quartz	22
Sunstone	24
Carnelian	26
Yellow Energy Mandalas of Crystals and Stones	29
Tigers Eye	30
Amber	32
Citrine	34
Green Energy Mandalas of Crystals and Stones	37
Amazonite	38
Malachite	40
Seraphanite	42
Moldavite	44
Pink Energy Mandalas of Crystals and Stones	47
Watermelon Tourmaline	48
Rose Quartz	50
Morganite	52
Rhodonite	54

Aqua Energy Mandalas of Crystals and Stones	57
Aquamarine	58
Turquoise	60
Chrysocolla	62
Larimar	64
Light Blue Energy Mandalas of Crystals and Stones	67
Angelite	68
Celestite	70
Blue Lace Agate	72
Indigo Blue Energy Mandalas of Crystals and Stones	75
Blue Kyanite	76
Sodalite	78
Lapis Lazuli	80
Purple Energy Mandalas of Crystals and Stones	83
Fluorite	84
Amethyst	86
White Energy Mandalas of Crystals and Stones	89
Flame of Ishtar	90
Selenite	92
Multi Colored Energy Mandalas of Crystals and Stones	95
Preseli Bluestone	96
Rainbow Moonstone	98
Rainbow Quartz	100
Labradorite	102
Epilogue	105

Introduction

As you can guess by the title of this book, I have an important partnership with crystals and stones as many of us do here on earth right now. I once heard that those of us who like to wear crystals are from Atlantis and we intuitively understand the energy and how to harness it. Crystals and stones have become such an integral part of who I am, so, of course I would create a book of the mandala energy of crystals and stones. The shear speed that some of these images came through was surprising. I created eighteen of these images in two days. . . interesting.

The first crystal I ever bought was actually a piece of jewelry. I did not know what I was buying. I was 12 years old and on a cruise with my family. We were in a jewelry store in St Thomas and I fell in love with this light blue stone in the shape of a sharks tooth. I could not stop starring at it and I knew I was supposed to have it. Years later, I found out it was Larimar. That was the first crystal/stone I ever bought and started a fascination with crystals and stones, which I still have today.

Other than jewelry the first crystal I purchased was a yellow calcite sphere. I was at an Expo and this crystal would not leave my hands. It was literally talking to me; I could feel the energy exchange between this crystal sphere and myself. I was fascinated and enthralled with it. The woman selling the sphere said it was obvious that this sphere was for you, and yes, it came home with me.

I would like to say my fascination with crystals and stones has lessened but it has not. I am sure I own enough to open my own store. Each one has a story and an energy that seems important to my journey. I feel the pull to bring them home,
and as I have mentioned do bring them home. Am I Hoarding or collecting? I have not decided as of yet.

Over the years I have had a visions of a healing room with crystals on different elevations to bring maximum effect. I know one day soon I will be able to create this healing space. I have also wanted to recreate the gates of Atlantis with the 144 spheres I am working on that as well. This project may take me a little longer to recreate.

What follows in this book are my interpretations of crystals and stones in the form of energy mandalas. I believe it is important to know what crystals do for you personally, not just what others' guidance has said. We are each unique and therefore will all interact differently with crystals and stones. For example, what ramps someone else up may actually calm them down and vice versa. So what follows are my interactions with each of the energy mandalas of crystals I have created. When you hold some stones and crystals they feel warm or hot whereas others feel cold, etc.

I have drawn and created all the mandalas in this book by hand; they are not computer generated. I have left the imperfections in, as that is how the originals look. I did enhance them by putting a glow around the image to help the image stand out a little.

Sit back and let yourself feel the power and majesty that crystals and stones have to offer. I hope you enjoy the ride. I know I have over the last 20 years of collecting them. Namaste!

Black and Red Energy Mandalas of Crystals and Stones

Hematite:

I use this stone for grounding, safety and protection. I love the shiny color of this stone and I can't help but wonder what the stone is absorbing or reflecting back to me when I hold it. Sometimes when I hold it I feel like I am being cleared and cleansed. Other times I feel like I am being charged or amped up. It just depends on what I need at the time.

Shungite:

This is a stone I have only picked up recently and the power in this stone is unbelievable. I have seen shungite for a long time and it never resonated with me until recently. I do not personally believe that shungite is of this world. Shungite helps me ground and connect multi dimensionally at the same time. It is an interesting experience to say the least.

Black Tourmaline:

I have used black tourmaline for grounding and helping myself clear negativity. When I work with people, this is often a stone I encourage them to get and to carry with them or place near them. I am a firm believer in the power of black tourmaline and what it can do. I feel like it is my own personal shield. Hence the shields in the design of this mandala.

Garnet:

I once had a garnet ring. I was fascinated by the dark richness of the red color and wanted to melt into it. Garnet helps me survive and thrive. It connects me to my passion and life force.

Orange Energy Mandalas of Crystals and Stones

Tangerine Quartz:

When I held tangerine quartz for the first time it literally brought a smile to my face. I felt a sense of joy and happiness in my being. Hence the smiley face in the middle. Tangerine quartz reminds me to not take life too seriously. It is okay to play, laugh, have fun and be silly.

Sunstone:

Sunstone brings a lightness of spirit and self.   Sunstone literally feels to me like I am harnessing the power of the sun and brining that energy into myself.   I can accomplish anything I dream I can do when I am working with sunstone.

Carnelian:

Carnelian is about connecting to who I am and what I want to put out in the world. I believe carnelian helps and works with me to increase my self worth and esteem. When I wear or carry carnelian helps me feel safe and secure in who I am.

Yellow Energy Mandalas of Crystals and Stones

Tigers Eye:

I have enjoyed Tiger's Eye and feet a pull to it. Tiger's eye reminds me to be fully in my power and to not make excuses for being in my power. Tiger's eye catches and commands it due to the shiny nature. I believe we are each unique and playing small does not serve anyone. I have learned that there is a difference between being in my power and being arrogant. I believe you can stay in your power and still be humble and Tiger's Eye helps me with this.

Amber:

Amber is a combination of who I am and being fully in my power. What a combination that is! I have many pieces of amber and even some green amber. I am fascinated by the messages it holds for me and my physical body. Not to mention all the messages it holds due to the ancient DNA and animals that have been encapsulated in it.

Citrine:

I love citrine all forms of citrine. Natural citrine and the yellow with a lot of white, and even the citrine with rainbows. Yes I did say rainbows; I have some citrine that does indeed have rainbows in it. Citrine helps me bring abundance into my life. It is a great stone to use for manifesting and being fully in your power.

Green Energy Mandalas of Crystals and Stones

Amazonite:

Amazonite helps me to calm down and feel peaceful especially when I am stressed. I find amazonite helps me self soothe. It just exudes a sense of quiet and peace, the feeling that everything is going to be okay.

Malachite:

Malachite is about balancing light and dark energies in your heart. It is about seeing both sides of yourself. Malachite helps me have compassion for myself from a heart space.

Seraphanite:

I enjoy the feel of seraphanite. It feels angelic and playful to me. Seraphanite helps me to be in joy, grateful and happy. I love to look at the green and white and see the interactions and the shapes it forms. Seraphanite helps me connect from my heart to other realms.

Moldavite:

Moldavite is a very powerful stone or tektite. It was deposited here on earth from a meteorite. Whenever I carry, wear or spray moldavite oil I am lifted higher and transported to another dimension. I believe moldavite helps me communicate from my heart multi dimensionally.

Pink Energy Mandalas of Crystals and Stones

Watermelon Tourmaline:

I find watermelon tourmaline to be loving and kind. Looking at watermelon tourmaline makes me happy, feel loved and joyful. It helps me connect those feelings to my heart center. Watermelon Tourmaline helps me to keep my heart and universal love in me balanced.

Rose Quartz:

Rose quartz is the stone most often associated with universal love. Rose quartz brings energy to help me deal with whatever is causing my stress. It reminds me to love my self about self-love and connect to the flow of universal love.

Morganite:

When I wear or think about morganite, I feel loved and cared for. I feel connected to this calm river of universal love that gently flows into me and washes away any sadness or loneliness.

Rhodonite:

Rhodonite helps me to ground love in the physical world. Rhodonite helps me work on accepting and loving myself as I am. I find that there are times I need a lot of work in this area. That is when I will wear or carry rhodonite with me.

Aqua Energy Mandalas of Crystals and Stones

Aquamarine:

I use aquamarine for centering and meditation. It helps me connect with my higher self, inner knowledge and wisdom. It brings this information forward in a gentle way. I feel ease with communicating when I work with aquamarine.

Turquoise:

Turquoise is kind of an all purpose stone. It helps on many different layers and levels. It is one of my go to stones. There is a reason that Native Americans have used turquoise in their jewelry and head pieces for as long as time exists. Turquoise helps with intuition and connecting to the earth and earth energies.

<u>Chrysocolla:</u>

Chrysocolla is great for creativity and bringing in ideas and balance. It helps me with expressing my creativity. When I am struggling artistically or with a project, I will turn to chrysocolla to help me think outside the box.

Larimer:

Larimar is one of my favorite stones and my first stone. I think of larimar as a feel good stone. For me, larimar holds the energy of wisdom, knowledge, dolphins and water. What could be better than that? Larimar is about being in joy and being present in the moment. Larimar provides me with a lightness of spirit.

Light Blue Energy Mandalas of Crystals and Stones

Angelite:

Angelite is a gift from the angelic realm. Angelite helps comfort me and leaves me full of grace. I love the feeling of peace and oneness I feel when I hold or carry angelite.

Celestite:

Celestite works to help calm me down. It has a soothing quality that can help me relax and emanates the energy of calmness.

Blue Lace Agate:

Blue lace agate opens my communication on all levels. It helps me balance my physical voice with my spiritual knowing, and trusting the messages I receive.

Indigo Blue Energy Mandalas of Crystals and Stones

Blue Kyanite:

I wore a piece of blue kyanite for a long time around my neck to help me feel confident in how I communicated. I found working with this stone helpful in the beginning of using my voice whether doing readings or speaking engagements. I think of blue kynatie as a Power Ranger for using my voice.

Sodalite:

Sodalite is a stone I have used a great deal. I have many spheres of sodalite. When I am working on anything that is going to involve my intuition and/or speaking I turn to sodalite to help. I find sodalite to be a gentle and powerful way to connect to my intuition.

Lapis Lazuli:

Lapis Lazuli is an ancient stone. It helps with my intuition and being open to my inner knowing. Lapis helps the messages I receive to be more grounded and fully experienced. I know that Lapis Lazuli was used a great deal in Egypt and Atlantis to help access intuition and holding visions. This has always been a very powerful crystal for me. Whenever I hold lapis I feel my third eye vibrate.

Purple Energy Mandalas of Crystals and Stones

Fluorite:

I have always enjoyed fluorite. The struggle for me is whenever I hold it I tend to crack it due to my energy field. I do have quite a bit of fluorite and love all the different color combinations and shapes it is available in. I find fluorite to be a more subtle stone to work with. I feel a sense of peace and connection when I work with it.

Amethyst:

Amethyst has always been one of my favorite stones. Anything purple is always good. When I work with amethyst I am flooded with information and feel an instant connection to all that is. I use amethyst and black amethyst a great deal when I am doing akashic record readings.

White Energy Mandalas of Crystals and Stones

Flame of Ishtar:
I find the flame of Ishtar interesting because whenever I look at it or hold it I enter a portal. I find this stone is good for traveling and having adventures. I also find this stone to carry light codes and helps me enter the world of light.

Selenite:

I have quite a collection of selenite. I am fascinated by how selenite looks and feels. I experience selenite as pure white light. I have used selenite to remove blockages or to clean and cleanse other stones. I find that I use a lot of selenite when I am designing crystal grids to hold the energy and space for the grid.

Multi Colored Energy Mandalas of Crystals and Stones

Preseli Bluestone:

Preseli Bluestone is an ancient stone, a building block of some of the ancient wonders of the world. I feel portals and gateways open when I hold this stone. I often feel an electric charge course through my body when I pick this stone up.

Rainbow Moonstone:

I love the magical quality of rainbow moonstone. I love the light that reflects off and forms the subtle colors. Moonstone to me is about going with the flow and rhythms of live.

Rainbow Quartz:

When I see the rainbows inside the quartz it always brings a smile to my face and lightness to my spirit. It helps soothe me in some ways and I feel a sense of peace. I love to connect to all the different energies that are present in rainbow quartz. I am open to receiving information that has been encoded in the quartz.

Labradorite:

I own a great deal of Labradorite. I cannot seem to get enough of the magical and protecting properties of labradorite. I love to look at all the colors and patterns when you move the stone in the light. The power in this stone is undeniable. I also wear labradorite and feel protected, magical and powerful. This is a multi purpose stone that I really enjoy.

Epilogue:

I hope you have enjoyed this journey into the world of crystals and stones through mandalas. I hope you have learned to trust your own intuition while picking out crystals and stones for yourself and what resonates with you. We all have the knowledge of how to do this. It is a matter of learning to trust your intuition and inner guidance.

www.ingramcontent.com/pod-product-compliance
Lightning Source LLC
Chambersburg PA
CBHW042138290426
44110CB00002B/54